NEPTUNE

MURRAY "OAK" TAPETA

NORWOOD HOUSE PRESS

Cataloging-in-Publication Data

Names: Tapeta, Murray.
Title: Neptune / Murray Tapeta.
Description: Buffalo, NY : Norwood House Press, 2026. | Series: Outer space | Includes glossary and index.
Identifiers: ISBN 9781978576476 (pbk.) | ISBN 9781978576483 (library bound) | ISBN 9781978576490 (ebook)
Subjects: LCSH: Neptune (Planet)--Juvenile literature.
Classification: LCC QB691.T374 2026 | DDC 523.48--dc23

Published in 2026 by
Norwood House Press
2544 Clinton Street
Buffalo, NY 14224

Copyright © 2026 Norwood House Press
Designer: Rhea Magaro
Editor: Kim Thompson

Photo credits: Cover, p. 1, 5, 7, 6, 18 NASA Images; pp. 8, 12, 1 3 buradaki/Shutterstock.com; p. 9 Andrij Vatsyk/Shutterstock.com; p. 11 Vadim Sadovski/Shutterstock.com; p. 14 Golubovy/Shutterstock.com; p. 15 winnond/Shutterstock.com; p. 17 Zongrit/Shutterstock.com; p. 21 Belish/Shutterstock.com;

All rights reserved. No part of this book may be reproduced in any form without permission in writing from the publisher, except by a reviewer.

Printed in the United States of America

Some of the images in this book illustrate individuals who are models. The depictions do not imply actual situations or events.

CPSIA compliance information: Batch #CSNHP26: For further information contact Norwood House Press at 1-800-237-9932.

TABLE OF CONTENTS

Where Is Neptune? 4

How Was Neptune Discovered? 8

What Is It Like on Neptune? 10

Has Neptune Been Explored? 19

Glossary 22

Thinking Questions 23

Index 24

About the Author 24

Where Is Neptune?

Our **solar system** has eight planets. Neptune is the farthest from the Sun. It is about four times as wide as Earth. You could fit 57 Earths inside Neptune!

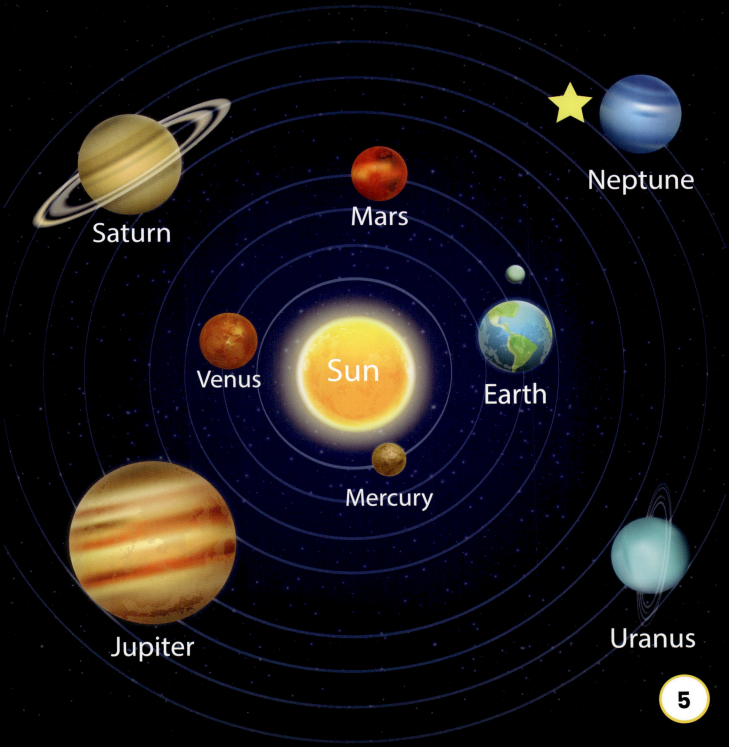

Neptune is about three billion miles (four and a half billion kilometers) from the Sun. The shortest trip to Neptune from Earth would take more than six years.

One year on Neptune lasts 60,190 Earth days. That is about 165 Earth years. It takes Neptune that long to **orbit** the Sun.

How Was Neptune Discovered?

Scientists looked at the way the planet Uranus moves. They predicted that our solar system had another planet. It was affecting Uranus.

German **astronomer** Johann Galle first saw Neptune through a **telescope** in 1846. Neptune was named after the Roman god of the sea.

What Is It Like on Neptune?

You could not stand on Neptune. It does not have a solid surface. It is made of flowing, icy materials. At its center is a rocky, Earth-sized **core**.

Neptune has 16 moons. At least five faint rings surround the planet.

The gas **methane** is in Neptune's **atmosphere**. It makes the planet look blue. Neptune is called "the blue giant."

13

Neptune is freezing cold. It is the windiest planet in our solar system. Winds blow as fast as 1,200 miles (1,900 kilometers) per hour.

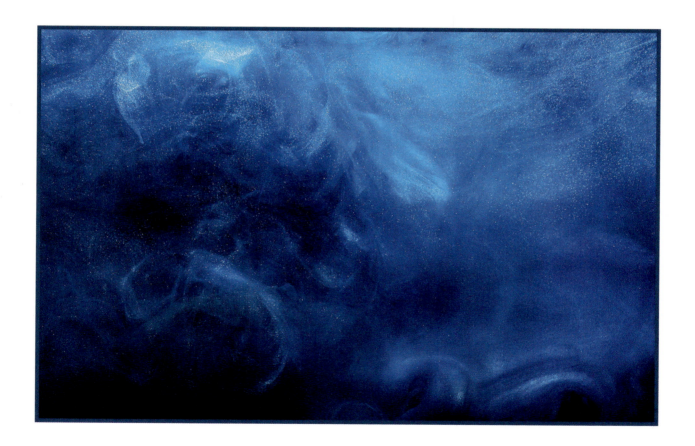

Gravity on Neptune is a little stronger than on Earth. If you weighed 100 pounds (45 kilograms) on Earth, you would weigh 110 pounds (50 kilograms) on Neptune.

Scientists think Neptune formed about five billion years ago. It started as a large spinning disk of dust, ice, and gas. Over time, it became a planet.

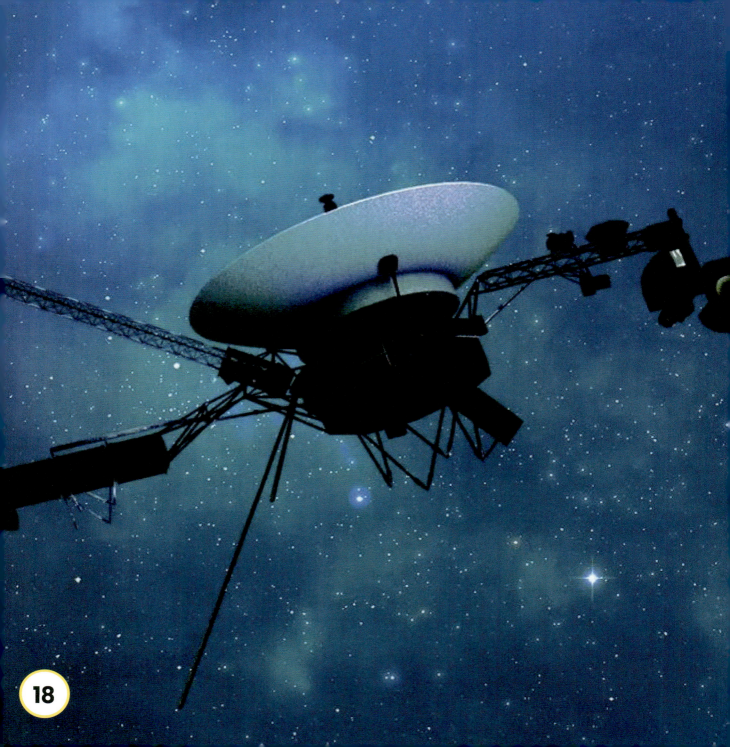

Has Neptune Been Explored?

Voyager 2 flew by Neptune in 1989. The **satellite** collected data. It sent pictures back to Earth. It is the only **spacecraft** that has come close to the planet.

Scientists want to send another mission to Neptune. Until then, they will use powerful telescopes to study the big blue planet at the edge of our solar system.

Glossary

astronomer (uh-STRAH-nuh-mer): a scientist who studies objects in the sky, including planets, galaxies, and stars

atmosphere (AT-muhs-feer): the mixture of gases that surrounds a planet; air

core (kor): most inner part; center

gravity (GRAV-i-tee): an invisible force that pulls objects toward each other and keeps them from floating away

methane (METH-ane): a colorless, odorless gas that burns easily

orbit (OR-bit): to follow a curved path around a larger body in space

satellite (SAT-uh-lite): a spacecraft sent into orbit around a planet, moon, or other object in space

solar system (SOH-lur SIS-tuhm): the Sun and everything that orbits around it

spacecraft (SPAYS-kraft): a vehicle that travels through space

telescope (TEL-uh-skope): an instrument that helps people see distant objects

Thinking Questions

1. How was Neptune discovered?

2. Describe the weather on Neptune.

3. Why does Neptune look blue?

4. How many moons orbit Neptune?

5. What satellite took pictures of Neptune?

Index

Earth 4, 6, 7, 10, 15, 19

Galle, Johann 9

gravity 15

moons 11

orbit 7

rings 11

Sun 4, 6, 7

surface 10

Voyager 2 19

wind 14

About the Author

Murray "Oak" Tapeta was born in a cabin without plumbing in Montana. Growing up in the great outdoors, he became a lover of nature. He earned the nickname "Oak" after climbing to the top of an oak tree at the age of three. Oak loves to read and write. He has written many books about events in history and other subjects that fascinate him. He prefers spending time in the wilderness with his dog Birchy.